To my Princesses Chloe and Mia,

that you may live a life worthy of our King.

COPYRIGHT © 2018
St Shenouda Press

All rights reserved. No part of this book may be reproduced in any manner without prior written permission from the publisher.

ST SHENOUDA PRESS
8419 Putty Rd,
Putty, NSW, 2330
Sydney, Australia

www.stshenoudapress.com

ISBN 13: 978-0-6482814-4-3

Once upon a time, there lived a girl named Demiana. She was a princess, born to a royal family. She had everything she ever wanted. Anything she asked for, she received. She had a huge room that was filled with so many exciting things. She also loved the large garden outside, where she would spend most of her time.

Demiana's father was a Christian. He always took her to Church. Demiana would hurry to Sunday School after the Liturgy because she loved to hear as much as she could about Jesus and the Saints. Demiana and her father would read the Bible together every night. She always had so many questions to ask about the Bible.

As Demiana grew older, her love for Jesus increased more and more. She spent a lot of time alone with Jesus. She did this by praying, reading the Bible, and obeying the commandments. Any chance she had, she would speak about Jesus. Those who worked around her home knew that she was a special girl.

One day when she was all grown up, her father came to her. "Demiana," he said, "We'll have to buy you a lovely white dress, for you are going to get married soon."

But Demiana became very sad at this news.

"Why are you so sad?" her father asked. "I only want to marry my heavenly Father, Jesus," Demiana replied, "I do not want to marry anyone else."

Her father tried to change her mind, but he could not. Demiana said, "Father, I want you to build me a palace out in the desert. I will spend all my time there with Jesus!" Her father was heartbroken. He also thought it was a dangerous thing to do. But since he could not change her mind, he finally agreed to do what she asked.

Her father built the palace and Demiana went to live there. Many girls began to hear about Demiana and also went to live with her. They too wanted to live only with Jesus. They became known as nuns. The nuns were so joyful to be able to spend their time in praise, holiness, and service. Together, their love for Jesus grew stronger and stronger every day!

One day while Demiana and the forty nuns were living in the palace praising God, they heard some horrible news. The wicked Emperor attacked Demiana's father as well as other Christians. The Emperor was angry because of their love and belief in Jesus. Many of them died and they were called Martyrs.

Soon, the Emperor found out that Demiana was living with forty nuns in the desert. He was furious that they spent all their time praying and loving Jesus. He ordered one of his commanders to take one hundred soldiers and attack the palace in the desert. The soldiers made the long and tiresome journey into the desert.

First, the Emperor tried to convince Demiana to worship idols. But she refused. He tried to talk to her about how great his idols were. She would not listen, so the Emperor began to hurt her. But every time the Emperor hurt her, Demiana looked to heaven and asked God for help. Whenever she prayed, God healed her. God was always with her.

The Emperor realised there was nothing more he could do. After trying to convince Demiana for a long time to worship the idols, he ended Demiana's earthly life. The forty nuns with her also refused to worship idols. So, the Emperor ended their lives too. Demiana and the nuns entered into the heavenly life where they became true brides of Jesus Christ. From then on, they would be known as Saint Demiana and the Forty Virgins.

THE END

www.ingramcontent.com/pod-product-compliance
Lightning Source LLC
LaVergne TN
LVHW072117070426
835510LV00002B/96